14 DAY

D0436171

If It Weren't For Farmers

By Allan Fowler

Consultants:

Robert L. Hillerich, Professor Emeritus,
Bowling Green State University, Bowling Green, Ohio
Consultant, Pinellas County Schools, Florida

Lynn Kepler, Educational Consultant

Fay Robinson, Child Development Specialist

Library of Congress Cataloging-in-Publication Data

Fowler, Allan.
    If it weren't for farmers/by Allan Fowler.
        p.   cm. — (Rookie read-about science)
    Summary: Briefly describes some of the work that is done on
different kinds of farms and the foods that are produced there.
    ISBN 0-516-06009-0
    1. Farmers—Juvenile literature. 2. Agriculture—Juvenile
literature. [1. Farms. 2. Food]
    I. Title. II. Series: Fowler, Allan. Rookie read-about science.

S519.F67 1993
630–dc20   92-35055
                                                               CIP
                                                               AC

If it weren't for farmers—

what would there be to eat?

All the fruits and vegetables,

all the milk and cheese,

meat and eggs you enjoy,

all the wheat that's made
into flour,

that's baked into bread and
cookies and cakes . . . all
of it comes from farms.

A farm is a place where people
work . . . to grow plants or
raise animals for food.

Some farm crops—such as oranges, grapefruits, and peaches—grow best where it's warm most of the time.

Others—such as apples
and berries, potatoes and
tomatoes—can be grown
in cooler climates.

And there are places where the soil and climate are just right for growing corn and grains.

Fields of wheat or corn stretch out as far as the eye can see.

Farmers often add fertilizer
to their soil. Fertilizer is plant
food. It helps farmers grow
bigger, healthier plants.

Many farmers use chemicals to kill harmful weeds and insects, and to protect the crops from plant diseases.

Other farms are organic.
They do not use chemicals.
They use only things found
in nature to help their
plants grow.

But the most important thing
all crops need is water.

Nothing can grow without water.
Sometimes there isn't enough rain.

Then the farmer irrigates his crops. He brings water to them from natural sources such as rivers or springs.

The water reaches the crops through an irrigation ditch, or

through a pipeline connected to sprinklers.

Today machines help the farmers
do their work.

Tractors pull the plows that break
up the soil . . . and the planters

that plant the seeds . . .
and the harvesters that gather
in the crops.

Some crops are so delicate that they would be crushed by machines. Raspberries, blueberries, and strawberries are like that, so they are picked by hand.

Besides crop farms, there are dairy farms where milk and cheese are produced . . .

poultry farms, where chickens
are raised for meat and eggs . . .

and cattle farms or ranches,
where cattle are raised for beef.

If it weren't for farmers —
what would there be to eat?

Words You Know

crop farms

fruits and vegetables

wheat

poultry farms

eggs

chickens

milk

dairy farms

cows

cattle ranch

organic farm

30

farm machines

tractor

plow

harvester

irrigation sprinklers

chemicals

Index

About the Author

Allan Fowler is a free-lance writer with a background in advertising. Born in New York, he lives in Chicago now and enjoys traveling.

Photo Credits

Grant Heilman Photography, Inc – ©Larry Lefever, 17, 30 (bottom right)

SuperStock International, Inc. – 6, 7, 13, 30 (top right, center left); ©Conrad Sims, Cover; ©Roy King, 3, 31 (top right); ©David Spindel, 4, 30, (top left); ©P. R. Productions, 5, 30 (center right center); ©Rivera Collection, 8; ©Schuster, 15, 31 (bottom right); ©Alan Briere, 21, 31 (bottom left); ©W. E. Ferguson, 23, 31 (center); ©Eric Carle, 27, 30 (center left center)

Valan – ©Francis Lépine, 9, 11; ©A. Scullion, 10, 20, 25; ©Jeannie R. Kemp, 14; ©John Cancalosi, 18; ©John Eastcott/Yva Momatiuk, 19; ©Kennon Cooke, 22, 29, 31 (top left); ©V. W.ilkinson, 26, 30 (center right); ©Ken Patterson, 28, 30 (bottom left)

COVER: Farm